Tiny Kushner

Five Plays

Tony Kushner

BROADWAY PLAY PUBLISHING INC
224 E 62nd St, NY, NY 10065
www.broadwayplaypub.com
info@broadwayplaypub.com

I S B N: 978-0-88145-627-1

First printing: June 2015
This printing: February 2016

Book design: Marie Donovan
Page make-up: Adobe Indesign
Typeface: Palatino
Printed and bound in the U S A

CONTENTS

CAST

ACTOR 1, *man, 20s: stage directions in* FLIP FLOP FLY!; BILLYGOAT *in* TERMINATING; *twenty-three different men and women in* EAST COAST ODE TO HOWARD JARVIS; *stage directions in* ONLY WE WHO GUARD THE MYSTERY SHALL BE UNHAPPY.

ACTOR 2, *man, 40s:* HENDRYK *in* TERMINATING; DR ARNOLD A HUTSCHNECKER in DR ARNOLD A HUTSCHNECKER IN PARADISE

ACTOR 3, *woman, 20s:* LUCIA PAMELA *in* FLIP FLOP FLY!; DYMPHNA *in* TERMINATING; *stage directions in* EAST COAST ODE TO HOWARD JARVIS; *and the* ANGEL *in* DR ARNOLD A HUTSCHNECKER IN PARADISE *and in* ONLY WE WHO GUARD THE MYSTERY SHALL BE UNHAPPY.

ACTOR 4, *woman, 30s-40s:* GERALDINE OF ALBANIA *in* FLIP FLOP FLY!; ESTHER *in* TERMINATING; METATRON *in* DR ARNOLD A HUTSCHNECKER IN PARADISE; *and* LAURA BUSH *in* ONLY WE WHO GUARD THE MYSTERY SHALL BE UNHAPPY.

FLIP FLOP FLY!

CHARACTERS

Actior 1
Lucia Pamela
Geraldine of Albania

(LUCIA PAMELA *is sitting alone, smiling, humming to herself.*)

ACTOR 1: A pretty lady with frizzled bangs and long corkscrew curls, dressed in a ball gown of synthetic taffeta, a rhinestone tiara on her head, a gaudy scepter in her gloved hands, is sitting on the rim of a tussock-sized meteor crater. Above her the sky is fathomless and black, filled with shockingly vivid stars. She is alone, but cheerful. Across her chest is a banner with glitter lettering: MISS ST. LOUIS, 1926.

This is the fabulous Lucia Pamela, American concert pianist, singer/songwriter, bandleader, radio-and-television personality. Although almost entirely forgotten at her death in 2002, Miss Pamela once had attained a minor degree of celebrity, when, in 1969, she released her album, *Into Outer Space With Lucia Pamela,* which she'd recorded earlier that year—

LUCIA: On the moon!

ACTOR 1: On the moon. Which is where (*He gestures to the lunar setting*) the action unfolds.

(ACTOR 1 *regards* LUCIA, *who stares out into space, smiling, humming to herself.*)

ACTOR 1: She is smiling, humming to herself. Suddenly, an enormous blood-red Mercedes limousine, vintage 1920s, six-foot-long hood, pulls up and idles, its supercharged engine filling the thin lunar air with diesel exhaust. As if by magic the passenger door of the red Mercedes opens.

(GERALDINE OF ALBANIA *enters.*)

ACTOR 1: A severely elegant woman steps out and surveys the landscape. She too wears a gown, she too has a crown, and she's bedizened with jewels, but unlike Miss Pamela's, these aren't ersatz. This is Geraldine, Queen of Albania, deposed and exiled in 1939 when Mussolini invaded her country. Like Lucia Pamela, Geraldine was virtually forgotten at the time of her death; she, too, died in 2002. Lucia died in July. Geraldine died in October. And the play takes place in November.

(LUCIA, *delighted, extends her hand.*)

LUCIA: Lucia Pamela, very pleased to meet you!

(GERALDINE, *not responding, recoils slightly.*)

LUCIA: I wish your driver'd turn off that engine, though. There's not a whole lot of air up here and—

GERALDINE: *(Peering in at the driver's seat:)* There doesn't appear to be a driver. *(She steps back, looks at the car.)* Oh. It's my car…

LUCIA: And it's a beaut! Like in the movies!

GERALDINE: Impossible. I haven't seen it in decades. We abandoned it, ages ago, the King my husband thought it too…recognizable. For our flight into exile.

LUCIA: You don't say!

GERALDINE: The car was a wedding present.

LUCIA: Wow! Some present! Who from?

GERALDINE: Hitler.

LUCIA: Hitler?!

GERALDINE: Yes, Hitler. Yes, that Hitler. Please tell me where I am. Is this… *(She reads* LUCIA's *banner.)* Saint Louis?

LUCIA: Gosh no! This is the moon!

ACTOR 1: Geraldine gets back in the Mercedes.

GERALDINE: I wish to leave at once. Please find my driver and instruct him to drive me back to Tirana.

LUCIA: Don't think you can leave, honey.

GERALDINE: Nonsense.

LUCIA: Nope. I never met Hitler but moon travel's something I know something about! Thirty years ago I came up here and recorded my famous album, *Into Outer Space With Lucia Pamela*. Two whole months before Neil Armstrong! It was my moonfriends who got me here and home again, and they're gone! Every one! I haven't seen so much as a single little Goony Goon! Of which there used to be several! The Goons, Moontown, it's just gone, like it never existed! So I dunno, but this visit feels kinda different, kinda permanent to me. But it's not so bad, it's quiet and peaceful, a little dusty, a little dry, a little lonely, no one to talk to or sing for—till now! See? You arrived! Company! Never be blue! Have a hap-hap-happy heart!

GERALDINE: You couldn't possibly have traveled here thirty years ago, you're barely twenty years old.

LUCIA: Oh honey, I only look twenty, how I looked when I won the title, the Miss Saint Louis beauty pageant. But I'm nintey-eight! Or I was. Now I'm just dead! Dead as a doornail!

GERALDINE: Dead as a what?

LUCIA: Doornail! It's an American expression. You aren't American are you?

GERALDINE: No.

LUCIA: Thought not.

(A beat, while GERALDINE *regards* LUCIA, *recognizing a displeasing quality.)*

GERALDINE: My mother was. American. Her name was (*With disgust:*) Gladys.

LUCIA: My mother was a very fine concert pianist! Paderewski told her I would grow up to be the world's greatest pianist. And Charles Kunkel, he was Beethoven's first cousin, he said—

GERALDINE: My father married far, far beneath himself. He was born Count Gyula Apponyi de Nagy Appony, descendant of the Arpadian Dynasty.

LUCIA: Wow.

GERALDINE: And I am the Queen of Albania.

LUCIA: And I am Marie of Rumania!

GERALDINE: Impostor! I knew Marie of Rumania!

LUCIA: No I was just making a joke! That's from a poem. I know ten thousand poems and songs. By heart! I was listed in *Ripley's Believe It or*—

GERALDINE: You are an entertainer?

(LUCIA *nods yes, vigorously.*)

GERALDINE: I am…dead?

(LUCIA *nods yes, sympathetically.*)

GERALDINE: I want to leave. I am Roman Catholic. Is this Purgatory? I don't want to be in Purgatory. For what, for marrying out of the Faith? I was penniless! And Zog was nobility! And I said Mass every morning! It's really too much. I don't want to be on the moon in Purgatory with a lunatic entertainer. Am I forever to be borne along, helplessly, debris adrift on the floodtide, at the mercy of every eddying current? Budapest, Tirana, Athens, London, Cairo, Paris, Madrid, Johannesburg, Tirana again, and, and…
I will go back to Albania. I returned once before, I can do it again. If Mussolini, Enver Hoxha, Ramiz Alia, that nasty business over illegal weapons in my Spanish

villa and a failed referendum for the restoration of the monarchy couldn't stop me, then what is the narrow sea that separates life from death? Let every doornail die! Tirana will see me again! Or my name isn't Geraldine of Albania.

LUCIA: Gee, that was a great speech. We could make a great song out of that speech! You want to do that? We got time, and I have my accordion!

ACTOR 1: Lucia Pamela reaches for her accordion.

GERALDINE: *(Appalled, imperiously:)* DON'T TOUCH IT.

ACTOR 1: Lucia Pamela ignores her and straps the accordion on.

LUCIA: I was a student at the Beethoven Music Conservatory in Germany, the greatest in Europe! When they heard me sing and play they said I was so advanced they had nothing to teach me. After that I won the Miss Saint Louis contest and the great Flo Ziegfeld asked me into his famous Follies! But instead I went touring with Charlie Kunkel, Beethoven's cousin, and we did piano-inventions-four-hands, like, everywhere! Charlie, he died at the keyboard one night, just slouched with a little chuffy noise, hit his noggin on the G above middle C, whammo, kaput! But I finished the concert, alone.

GERALDINE: None of that is true!

LUCIA: That was before I flew to the moon and made my famous record, *Into Outer—*

GERALDINE: You are insane. You make these things up. You…self-dramatize. If we are to spend the countless hours between now and Judgment Day together, here in Purgatory, you must not do that. It offends.

LUCIA: Don't see why it should.

GERALDINE: Because some of us have lived lives
of real hardship! I was born a Countess, reduced
to selling postcards in Budapest. I had to leave my
indigent family, travel to Albania, learn how to
conquer the hearts of my people, Muslims distrustful
of a Roman Catholic and a Hungarian, and I did it! I
saw my husband, my people seduced and betrayed
by Mussolini! I fled over the mountains into Greece
pursued by Italian soldiers still bleeding from
childbirth.

LUCIA: The soldiers were bleeding from childbirth???!!!!

GERALDINE: NO YOU IDIOT!! I, I!! I fled over the
mountains bleeding!

LUCIA: I married a prizefighter.

GERALDINE: I was menaced in Greece, mocked in
London by the effeminate British! "King Zog's Circus"
they called us!

LUCIA: The prizefighter, he was my fourth or fifth
husband. Or sixth. He was a palooka!

GERALDINE: The happy times in Egypt, till the fickle
Egyptians deposed their king! The lonely days of
widowhood in France, after my Zogu died!

LUCIA: And speaking of France, back in 1969 I found
a village on the moon inhabited by walking talking
pecans and walnuts, if you can believe that, and they
spoke French! Turns out the French colonized the
moon years before—

GERALDINE: The warmth and generosity of
Generalissimo Franco, my comfortable home in
Madrid, surrounded by priests!

LUCIA: I played fifteen instruments! I had the first all-
girl orchestra, Lucia Pamela and The Musical Pirates!
My daughter and I had a duo, The Pamela Sisters, she
was my daughter but I looked young enough to—

GERALDINE: The tender maternal hopes I had for my
Leka, my only son, his grenade launchers hidden in the
wine cellar, his flight to Johannesburg, the ingratitude
of his people, rejecting their king. And then that
bittersweet invitation, from the "Parliament" in Tirana:
The Albanian people invite their Queen to come home.
Come home... Impaupered. Bereft of jewels and title.
To die...

LUCIA: Are those jewels real? I been meaning to ask
but—

GERALDINE: OF COURSE THEY'RE REAL! MY
HUSBAND ZOG THE FIRST OF ALBANIA CARRIED
THEM ACROSS THE MOUNTAINS. Then we... We
pawned them, but... They're back. In Purgatory I have
my jewels again.

LUCIA: I don't know where you came up with this
Purgatory business, honey, your Royal Highness, this
is just the moon, the round old moon, a little lacking in
creature comfort but a jolly old moon regardless, you
should get a brighter outlook! I used to be the host of
a show on radio called *The Encouragement Hour* and
every day—

GERALDINE: This is what offends! Galls! Grates on
the nerves! Americans! You make up these fantastic
stories! These idiotic invented lives! My life is the
collapse of the Austro-Hungarian Empire! My life
is the frustrated dream of the Albanian people of
Albania, Kosovo, Montenegro, for the establishment
of Greater Albania! My life in the terminus-heap of
the struggles of the Ottoman Empire to invade the
West, the West's attempts to invade the East, the clash
between Islam and Christianity, my life is the Balkans,
my life is a mountainous centuries-old tragedy, my
life is the story of Fascism's promise and its betrayal,
of the appalling, disastrous European flirtation with

democracy, my life is secret armament caches and
the perdurable lust-dreams of deposed kings for their
stolen patrimonies, my life is hostage to the vain dream
of autarky and its twisted diplomacy, one million
Albanians and eight hundred million Chinese in league
against Soviet aggression, while you— You're just like
MOTHER! Gladys Virginia Stewart, American! All
fantasy and pretension so she marries a Count, not
bothering to notice HE'S BROKE!! She'd have done
better to fly to the moon and marry a French-speaking
walnut! AMERICANS! NO SENSE OF HISTORY! NO
SENSE OF TRAGEDY! EVERYTHING WILL HAVE
ITS HAPPY ENDING! And it's the daughters who are
left to suffer the reality!

LUCIA: My daughter owns the Saint Louis Rams.

GERALDINE: The… What? What on earth are you—

LUCIA: So you see, everything turned out O K! And
you know what, gee, I don't know, I don't even know
who half the people you talk about are, but you and
me, we both had fantastical lives, just fantastical—

GERALDINE: But…mine happened!

LUCIA: *(Enthusiastic agreement:)* I bet!

GERALDINE: It actually happened—

LUCIA: *(More enthusiastic agreement:)* Uh huh! But you
know—

GERALDINE: But nothing!

LUCIA: I was just—

GERALDINE: NO BUTS! NO BUTS! IT HAPPENED,
IT HAPPENED, MY LIFE OCCURRED, TOOK
PLACE, TRANSPIRED AS I HAVE DECSRIBED IT,
IN ACTUALITY, IN HISTORY, IN TIME, TICKING
TOCKING TIME, ACTUAL HISTORICAL RECORDED
MINUTES AND AND— *(Continuous with line below:)*

LUCIA: *(Happily to herself:)* Tick tock, kookoo clock! Tick tock, kookoo clock!

GERALDINE: *(Continuous from above:)* —HOURS AND DAYS AND YEARS OF MEASURABLE, OF OF…

(GERALDINE stops, powerless to dent LUCIA's imperturbable smile. LUCIA, delighted by all the noise and passion, waits for GERALDINE to go on; GERALDINE can't. Then:)

LUCIA: Of what, honey?

GERALDINE: *(Uncertainly:)* It, it happened, you spectacularly ignorant oblivious— It… *(Almost pleading:)* Did.

LUCIA: But even so, you know, it sounds like the plot for a T V movie!

GERALDINE: *(Near tears, needy:)* It…does?

LUCIA: Uh huh! Or a play! A musical comedy play! We could make one up! I can do tunes on the accordion and you can rhyme stuff. I remember a musical play on Broadway once about a lady who was gorgeous the way you are, and she ran a country and was even friends with some dictator, like you! Eva somebody. And her musical was the hugest hit, they made a movie movie out of it, with that singer, oh, the one with just one name, you know, you know the one I mean? It's on the tip of my—

GERALDINE: Madonna.

LUCIA: YES! She's the Lucia Pamela of her day, she may not be the best actress but she believes in herself and when you do that, everything's possible, you just gotta believe! That's what it means to be American! Believe! And we can make a play like that, of your life, Geraldine! It rhymes with, with… Queen! Because life's just a lot of made up stuff, isn't it? And every hour can be Encouragement Hour, can't it? And a girl's gotta dress for the occasion, no matter what! Gotta do up the curls and pick up the accordion and sing sing sing.

GERALDINE: When you were alive, did you ever consider running a Pyramid Scheme?

LUCIA: You mean like King Tut?!

GERALDINE: You'd have managed very well in Albania.

LUCIA: Never made it to Albania. I played Albany once!

GERALDINE: Close enough.

LUCIA: Great! Let's start our musical with a song I already wrote, it's from my famous album *Into Outer Space With Lucia Pamela.*
I'll begin and you sing along.

GERALDINE: I can't sing.

LUCIA: So? You think I let that stop me? Not for a minute!
We're going to do a dance and a song! *The Flip Flop Fly!*
When I say flip, you flip! When I say flop, you flop!
When I say fly… We'll all fly!

(LUCIA *plays her accordion, joined by an invisible klezmer band! She sings:*)

LUCIA: Flip flop fly,
flip flop fly,
You flip, I'll flop, we'll both fly!
Flip flop fly,
now you're my guy,
let's all try to do the flip flop fly!
Go man go,
Oh! Oh! Oh!
We're all doin' the flip flop fly!
Flip flop fly,
flip flop fly,
way up in the sky!

Up in outer space we'll go,
where the winds so softly blow,
through the clouds, hangin' low,
touchin' the stars,
Jupiter and Mars,
Go man go,
Oh! Oh! Oh!
We're all doin' the flip flop fly!
Flip flop fly,
You're my guy,
It's just time to do the flip flop fly!
(To GERALDINE:*)*
SING WITH ME!

*(*GERALDINE *joins in, reluctantly, tentatively, trying to keep up, doing better and better as the song progresses:)*

GERALDINE & LUCIA: *(Singing:)*
Flip flop fly,
flip flop fly,
You flip, I'll flop, we'll both fly!
Flip flop fly,
You're my guy,
Way up in the sky!

(Dance break! They dance! LUCIA *does a simple tap dance step.* GERALDINE *imitates it awkwardly.* LUCIA *shows it again,* GERALDINE *picks it up, and then they're off, tapping together, better and better.* GERALDINE *adds a quick elaboration that looks like goose-stepping with a fascist salute,* LUCIA *right behind her! Then back to the tap dance for the BIG FINISH!)*

LUCIA: *(Singing, with a sudden vehemence!)*
NO MORE TAXES NO MORE BILLS!!

GERALDINE & LUCIA: *(Singing:)*
Just doin' the flip flop fly!
Then we'll fly to the moon!

Whee!
DOIN' THE FLIP! FLOP! FLY!

END OF PLAY

TERMINATING
OR
SONNET LXXV
OR
"LASS MEINE SCHMERZEN NICHT
VERLOREN SEIN"
OR
AMBIVALENCE

CHARACTERS

ACTOR 4
HENDRYK
ESTHER
DYMPHNA
BILLYGOAT

ACTOR 4: Esther is an analyst, and this is her office: a chair and a couch. Hendryk sits on the couch, he does not lie on the couch. Esther is nicely turned out, Hendryk is a godforsaken mess. Dymphna, Esther's younger domestic partner, sits in a chair near Esther, and Billygoat, Hendryk's erstwhile much-more-attractive lover, sits near the couch, though neither Dymphna nor Billygoat is, in fact, in the office.

HENDRYK: I've gained twenty-four pounds.

ESTHER: Hendryk.

HENDRYK: Last night on the subway I urinated.

ESTHER: Hendryk.

HENDRYK: In my pants.

ESTHER: Hendryk.

HENDRYK: Bladder, um, bladder control, loss of, sudden loss of… Waters breaking, whoosh! Drenched!

ESTHER: Hendryk.

HENDRYK: I'm broke.

ESTHER: Hendryk.

HENDRYK: I spent all my money on these…these…these…

ESTHER: Hendryk.

HENDRYK: I…

(HENDRYK *waits for the "Hendryk." It doesn't come.*)

HENDRYK: I, I didn't *need* them, it was just, they're…. Drapes. It was an idea I had, to, to sew real, uh real, uh actual chicken feathers—

ESTHER: Hendryk.

HENDRYK: Quilted, sort of, big squares between sheets of sheer, um, *raw*…silk. *(He waits for the "Hendryk". It doesn't come so he says:)* Hendryk.
I find I'm saying *raw* a lot these days, raw silk, raw… um, burlap steak wound meat eat me raw the, the raw truth. Raw and, um, *rank*. Rank…*betrayal*.

ESTHER: Hen—

HENDRYK: All this coil is long of you. Mistress. As they say. *RAW*. Not like I'm not perfectly contented to be free of this room and the constraints of your ultimate indifference to the, uh, the uhhhhh, the.

(Pause)

ESTHER: Hendryk.

HENDRYK: I want to come back.

ESTHER: No.

HENDRYK: Why not?

ESTHER: I…

HENDRYK: Why?

ESTHER: We terminated.

HENDRYK: So?

ESTHER: You…
Because.

HENDRYK: What?

ESTHER: You frighten me.

HENDRYK: You're not supposed to say things like that. You're not supposed to say anything, really.

ESTHER: I can say anything I want, Hendryk, you're not my patient anymore.

HENDRYK: But still.

ESTHER: Well you do frighten me.

HENDRYK: I am in love with you.

ESTHER: Transference.

HENDRYK: I don't believe in transference.

ESTHER: Uh huh.

HENDRYK: *All* love is transference. Breast, mom, every fucking other fucking—

ESTHER: Hendryk.

HENDRYK: I love you.

ESTHER: Hendryk, you do not, I mean—

HENDRYK: I do. It's not—

ESTHER: Hendryk, I—

HENDRYK: —transference.

ESTHER: I HAVE PROBLEMS OF MY OWN, HENDRYK! PROBLEMS! PROBLEMS!

DYMPHNA: I thought you terminated with him. Tell him to leave. Is it bad today?

HENDRYK: This isn't going well and perhaps I should...

(Pause)

ESTHER: I should not have said that you frighten me.

HENDRYK: Countertransference.

ESTHER: Well...

HENDRYK: Unanalyzed countertransference. *(Pause)* What?

ESTHER: It...

HENDRYK: Oh. It's...*not* counter... So, it's...what? *Reality?*

ESTHER: Hendryk.

HENDRYK: I am, I mean I actually *am... Frightening?* I mean, *me?*

(Pause)

HENDRYK: I. Um. The. Um. A-ha. A...ha. Wow.

ESTHER: How would it make you feel if I said you were frightening?

HENDRYK: But you did say that.

ESTHER: And how did—

HENDRYK: No if.

ESTHER: But how—

HENDRYK: No hypothetical.

ESTHER: But.

HENDRYK: You *said* it.
Sleep with me. At least.

ESTHER: *(Laughs)* You're gay.

HENDRYK: Oh yeah, well, so what. Gay. What. Is. That. You're a dyke, I'm gay, so...

ESTHER: Actually I never said I was a—

HENDRYK: Oh come on.

ESTHER: What?

HENDRYK: You wear...*Harley Davidson boots* and you have short hair.

ESTHER: Once I wore those boots.

HENDRYK: We saw each other for—

ESTHER: You were my patient.

HENDRYK: I...what?

ESTHER: We didn't "see" each other.

HENDRYK: For five years.

ESTHER: You make it sound like we dated.

HENDRYK: You think this is all about my mother.

ESTHER: It's not *not* about your mother. Of course I think it's about—

HENDRYK: I think you're a dyke.

ESTHER: Lesbian.

HENDRYK: Wasn't hostile.

ESTHER: Felt like it.

DYMPHNA: *(To* ESTHER:*)* Thought he was gone.

ESTHER: *(To* DYMPHNA:*)* He's supposed to be.

BILLYGOAT: *(To* HENDRYK:*)* So are you to my thoughts as food to life.

HENDRYK: *(To* BILLYGOAT:*)* Stop it. *(To* ESTHER:*)* I've gained twenty-four pounds.

BILLYGOAT: Or as sweet-seasoned showers are to the ground.

HENDRYK: Last night on the subway I urinated. In my pants.

BILLYGOAT: And as for the peace of you I hold such strife—

HENDRYK: *(To* BILLYGOAT:*)* SHUT UP! I hate the sonnets. Boring boring boring.

BILLYGOAT: —as 'twixt a miser and his wealth is found.

HENDRYK: I'm BROKE! I know women who have slept with you. New York is a tiny village. Well, it isn't but I do. I work with a woman who has. Slept with you.

ESTHER: No you don't.

HENDRYK: Yes I do.

ESTHER: No you don't.

HENDRYK: Yes I do. I know you're a lesbian.

ESTHER: And how does it make you feel.

HENDRYK: Sleep with me.

ESTHER: I'm going to charge you for this visit.

HENDRYK: I'll pay twice what I paid.

ESTHER: You're broke.

HENDRYK: I'll mug someone.

ESTHER: Ba-DUM-bump.
You keep saying "sleep" with me.

HENDRYK: Sex.

ESTHER: Sleep isn't sex.

HENDRYK: Nitpicker.

ESTHER: It's interesting.

HENDRYK: Kleinian nitpicker. I think you can sleep
with me, uh, have sex with me because unlike the truly
great analysts of the past who had unshakeable faith in
the stern tenets of their discipline you and all modern
practitioners of…well, of anything, of psychoanalysis
in this instance, in our…um, *pickle*, conundrum,
whatchamacallit, have, well, faith but no unshakeable
faith, no one does in anything these days, we have…
ambivalence, it's why we tattoo ourselves.

ESTHER: What?

HENDRYK: So like those priests who wind up sleeping
with children, it's not their fault, I mean we should
put them in prison of course kill them probably who
knows I know that's bad to say but there are days
when everyone, um seems like everyone should be
killed, you know? In a world in which no structure
rests assuredly, with assurancy on a foundation, in
which nothing comes with a metaphysical guarantee,

because even, take even an old atheist like Freud, God
was still *watching*, He was *watching* all the way up until
so-on-and-so-forth but today, today… Well take me for
instance.
Only you have ever been watching me. For five years.
And nothing lasts longer than five years. Used to
be, used to be…*ten* at least. And so abuse of your…
of *one's*…wards, patients, *inferiors*, subjects. Well it's
wrong but not absolutely so because there simply are
no absolutes, and. The, uh.

ESTHER: I think the associative leap to tattoos is
interesting.

HENDRYK: Tattoos last.

ESTHER: Your mother was tattooed.

HENDRYK: *That* again.

ESTHER: I am *absolutely* never going to sleep or have sex
with you.

HENDRYK: Because I'm fat, urinate in my pants, and I'm
broke. And frightening. I have a thought disorder.

ESTHER: I don't think you do.

HENDRYK: I think I do, but perhaps my thinking I do is
a result of a thought disorder. If you think you have a
thought disorder and you do have one, you're thinking
a correct thought, in which case you don't have a
thought *disorder*. So if I *don't* have a thought disorder,
but think I do, *that is* a disorder, which means I *do* but
then well you get the point. It's a small point. I saw a
man with tatoos all over his body yesterday covering
almost all his flesh like an epidermatological crisis.
Now *that's* frightening. And I thought wow, the uh.
Bet his skin will always smell like cheap ink. I thought,
wow, the *pain*, he must've really enjoyed that suffering,
bet he remembers every inky little needle stick. This
is how he knows he's been here. Because it hurt to be.

He has inscribed proof of his, well, not *existence* but...
O K, sure, existence, sure, existence in, inscribed on his
own, on his, in the only arena available to the late 20th
Century Citizen seeking effectivity, historical agency:
his or her skin. I cannot change any world except
this small world which is bounded by my skin. I can
change nothing, I can only hire a biker with a needle to
bruise into my flesh, "Live Free or Die."
I'm scared. I'm scared of the world.
I really want to come back to you.
Maybe I'll get a tattoo.
(Pause)
Ambivalence expands our options. It increases our
freedom, to, to... tattoo. Our selves. If we wish to. To
have a concept like "our selves" or "my self." Which
makes us more ambivalent and more free. Which
drives us crazy, and makes us desperate to find non-
ambivalent things like tattoos which for all their
permanence and pain serve mainly as markers of how
ambivalent and impermanent we are. Or feel we are.

ESTHER: Actually tattoos are removable. Nowadays.

HENDRYK: I hate the way you introduce irrelevancies.
(Pause)
I have a boyfriend now.

ESTHER: That's good.

HENDRYK: He's beautiful and he has no soul. None. In
nature there's no deformity but the mind. None are
called evil but the unkind. Beauty's, um, good, a good
thing, beauty is goodness, but the Beauteous Evil are
empty trunks o'erflourished by the whatchamacallit.
The Devil. As they say.
I don't, I don't by the way believe that you are right
that my mother named me Hendryk because it sounds
like Schmendrick.

SHE WAS DUTCH. FOR CHRIST'S SAKE! It's a
DUTCH NAME! NOT…um, NOT. BECAUSE. IT
SOUNDS. LIKE SCHMENDRIK. I don't think she
meant that. I think that's wrong. I think you could
be, uh I could sue you for malpractice for suggesting
that, for, for, implanting, inscribing whatchamacallit,
for forging neural pathways in my brain. Maternal
ambivalence is lethal. You ruined my life.

ESTHER: But she did call you Schmendrik, Hendryk.

HENDRYK: SO?

ESTHER: She called you that all the time. It's Dutch but
you were born in Massapequa. Schmendrick, Hendryk.
The words are practically homonymic.

HENDRYK: Homophonous, actually, is what you—

ESTHER: Homonym and homophone are…
homologues. They're homologous.

HENDRYK: They're homonyms, actually, not
homologues, though homophony is the precise—

ESTHER: But if they're homonymous then they're
precisely—

HENDRYK: Though there is a word more precisely
connoting closeness but imprecision. But I can't
remember what it is. Homophones are, like—

ESTHER: Tattoo and taboo.

HENDRYK: No, those aren't, they're, oh ha ha.
My mom's favorite actor was Oskar Homolka. When
she was angry she'd say "What have you done, Oskar
Homolka?" "Listen up, Oskar Homolka!" The subtext
of the last minute is "homosexual". There I beat you to
it. Pissed?
All this coil is long of you.
I want back in.

Tattoos are taboo for Jews. Taboo. It's….
TABOOOOOOOOOOOOOOOOoooooooooo. Like anal
sex. I'm not a homosexual. I can't be. I have no talent to
be. And anyway, the, uh. Anal sex disgusts me. Ugh.
Anal sex. Ugh. I am filled with horror. Well that's too
strong. Disgust.

BILLYGOAT: Do you know why that is?

HENDRYK: I don't know why it doesn't disgust
everyone.

BILLYGOAT: But it doesn't.

HENDRYK: I don't know why.

BILLYGOAT: All sex has fragrance, and is sometimes
malodorous. Love like Attar of Rose overwhelms
with its fierce volatility the mephitic pungency
of elimination and waste. When two lovers are
conjoining. When my cock is up your butt.

HENDRYK: That is horribly horribly horribly
embarrassing, what you just said, and I am going to
vomit.

BILLYGOAT: Shit transforms.

HENDRYK: No it doesn't. It's irreducibly revolting.
And germy. That is its essence. To revolt, and spread
disease. You are very beautiful but you have no soul.

BILLYGOAT: Shit transforms when you're in love.

HENDRYK: Maybe I've never been in love.

BILLYGOAT: Maybe not.

(Pause)

HENDRYK: How…sad.

ESTHER: Schmendrik.

HENDRYK: *(To* ESTHER:*)* Waitaminnit. *(To* BILLYGOAT:*)*
But you love me.

BILLYGOAT: I do.

HENDRYK: But how is that possible? I mean, *look at me*? And you have no soul. I, I'm reasonably sure about that. You're a satyr. A Priapist. Nothing human is alien to you. It's inhuman.

BILLYGOAT: Having no soul makes a person indiscriminate. Makes it possible to fall in love with unworthy object choices, like you.

HENDRYK: But if I don't let you fuck me, you'll leave me.

DYMPHNA: I thought he was gone, I thought he terminated.

ESTHER: He asked to see me.

DYMPHNA: What's his real name? *(Pause)* I hate him. You shouldn't let him back.

ESTHER: I won't.

DYMPHNA: Ever. Promise.

ESTHER: Ever. Banished. Be gone.

HENDRYK: I don't understand.

BILLYGOAT: I have to leave you.

HENDRYK: But that's...that's *crazy*. You love me so much my shit smells like attar of rose. I mean I can't even say that without feeling nausea. But you say it does. But you're going to leave me if we don't fuck.

BILLYGOAT: Yes. Because your refusal means you don't love me. I know that's bad to say but we both know what the refusal means. You don't love me, Hendryk. And that breaks my heart. It makes me want to die.

HENDRYK: So if you leave me, you're going to die? Or are you just going to find a boyfriend who has no problems with the smell of attar?

BILLYGOAT: Ummmm. The latter.

ESTHER: This morning I thought the bed was full of sand.

HENDRYK: I don't understand.

DYMPHNA: Is it bad today?

ESTHER: Hi-ho hi-ho it's off to work I go.
Yes, it's very very bad.
I want to die. God has closed my womb and I want to die. As a lesbian and a feminist and a rational progressive person and everything I am, as lucky as I am, I know it's bad to say this but I don't give a fuck, I am so fucking depressed I want to die. Die die die die die die die. I want to have a baby. If I can't have a baby I want to die. I can't take any more of those pills, I don't want to get cancer; I don't want to superovulate I just want to have a baby so bad I want to die but I don't want cancer. But I really do want to die. I hate the baby that won't be born. I hate the five failed sperm donors. Inexplicably, I hate you. Certainly I hate myself. I can't describe the hatred I feel for the doctors who…I have projected the hatred I feel for those doctors and their superovulators onto my shrink and her antidepressants so I can't remember to take my Zoloft, which I need to do but I hate her and her Zoloft for seeking to rob me of my death—desiring depression which is now the only thing left of my baby. I don't believe in God, I never did, not even a little but my hate believes in God apparently and He has closed my womb so fuck God. While my patients are jabbering away on the couch I wish I had a big sand bucket like kids have at the beach and I imagine myself with a plastic shovel pouring sand in their jabbering mouths, slowly and deliberately and seriously the way kids do, filling their mouths with sand not just to (*To* HENDRYK:) SHUT THEM UP (*To* DYMPHNA:) but obviously to strangle them; I wish all the world was burnt to a cinder, I wish I lived on the Island of Montserrat. I do live on the

Island of Montserrat. You know that island with the…
whatchamacallit, um, *volcano.* I imagine you calling
my patients and saying "Esther is dead, Doctor Zauber
is dead, she killed herself, sorry, here are referrals,"
they would all be shocked and sad and so forth but
also deeply gratified to have finally heard what you
sound like, to have it confirmed that you exist, *my lover.*
Parasites. Oy. Oy. Die. Die. Oy vey iz mir. Oh woe is
me. Every morning's…I'm sorry, but it's only ever
"Oh no not *this* again." And know what? My complete
lack of hope is all that keeps me alive. I think that if for
one moment I felt hope, I would have the courage kill
myself. For real.

BILLYGOAT: *(To* HENDRYK:*)* There's always douching.

ESTHER: *(To* HENDRYK:*)* Did you ever play on the shore
with a sand bucket?

HENDRYK: *(To* ESTHER:*)* Why? *(To* BILLYGOAT:*)*
Douching isn't foolproof.

ESTHER: Just wondering.

BILLYGOAT: Ah, well, *foolproof.*

HENDRYK: I hate that.

BILLYGOAT: What?

HENDRYK: That continental wearywise affected
sophisticated louche thing you lapse into. Ah well,
foolproof. Americans don't say "Ah". Ah well,
foolproof. Ah well the smell of feces. In the faubourg
of Paree of my youth we would eat it with petit-pois
off tiny platters of Limoges… Please. You're from
Dearborne. In houses all across Dearborne mothers are
teaching little boys to crinkle their noses in revulsion
at the smell of ordure. Maybe they don't even need
instruction, maybe it's innate, atavistic: Poo-poo, yuck.
What went wrong with you?

BILLYGOAT: With love's light wings did I o'erperch that revulsion.

HENDRYK: You're so *robust*. You don't really *get* ambivalence. The satyr which is half man half goat should get ambivalence but animals don't, that's why we say they have no souls, ambivalence is the soul, it is our species being, and against animal certitude human ambivalence is too ambivalent to stand up for itself I guess and so, voila. You. I'm going to lie down now.

ESTHER: Time's almost up.

HENDRYK: *(To* ESTHER:*)* Can I fuck you?

DYMPHNA: *(To* ESTHER:*)* Can I fuck you?

BILLYGOAT: *(To* HENDRYK:*)* Can I fuck you?

ESTHER: *(To* HENDRYK:*)* No. *(To* DYMPHNA:*)* No fucking tonight.

BILLYGOAT: Don't let me leave you. I may not have a soul but I'm beautiful so do your soul a favor, hang on tight to me.

HENDRYK: I'm going to lie down now.

ESTHER: When you lie down on the couch you always pass out. Your efficient Resistance.

HENDRYK: Just for a… *(He lies down.)* For old times's sake. To what? Why resist. I never met anyone who wasn't overcome. Eventually.
The pillow always smells.

ESTHER: Many troubled heads have been laid upon it. What about paternal ambivalence?

(HENDRYK *buries his face in the pillow and inhales deeply.)*

ESTHER: What does it smell like, Hendryk?

HENDRYK: Attar. Of Something. Nice.
Not now I'm trying to sleep.

(A little pause)

ACTOR 4: Esther fishes the keys to her office out of her purse, then scribbles something on a piece of paper. She wraps the keys in the paper, puts them quietly on the sleeping Hendryk's chest, turns out the lights and tiptoes out.

ACTOR 2: Hendryk wakes up as the door shuts. He looks about. He sits up. The paper enfolding the keys falls into his lap. He unfolds the paper; he jingles the keys. He reads the note.

(A little pause, and then, as HENDRYK:*)*

Lock. Up. After. Yourself.

END OF PLAY

Thank you for seeing me. Aren't I sad? Paternal ambivalence, there's no such thing as that. My father lacked ambivalence. He hated me, till he figured out how to swallow me. Which he did in three snaps of his mighty jaws, and washed me down with beer. It hardly hurt. Him or me. Once incorporated I was more or less safe. Though...
(He's getting sleepy.)
...spectacularly, lipsmackingly, invincibly... unappetizing.
Ready to be...extruded... Which... hah. Might be the key, a key to my, uh, horror of...shit...
(He's asleep.)

ESTHER: Hendryk.
Hendryk.
I have problems of my own.

DYMPHNA: Our inability to love one another is humankind's greatest tragedy. Why can't people live up to their moral goodness? It's better to share. It's more pleasant to be kind. Maybe not in the moment, but immediately after. It's exhausting to despair. Love replenishes itself, day after day.
It's easy to love, it's hard to refuse. Surprises are always coming. Adversity is better met by good cheer and a placid spirit. Generosity makes us free. Sacrifice lifts the soul. For the happy woman there is no terror in the night. *Lass meine Schmerzen nicht verloren sein.* Let my sorrow and my pain not be in vain. Don't kill yourself. Work. Each evening come home to me. Surely goodness and mercy will follow me all the days of my life. I love that. Surely they shall. Surely. Surely.

ESTHER: For me that word is so rotten with doubt and hesitation, it rings. It's a question in a closet.

DYMPHNA: Don't kill yourself. Work. Every evening come home to me.

EAST COAST ODE TO HOWARD JARVIS

A little teleplay in tiny monologues

CHARACTERS

ACTOR 3
ACTOR 1

Author's note: I think this will work best with one actor playing all the parts. The actor could be a woman or a man. The interior and exterior titles, character descriptions and character indentifications should be spoken by the actor before each character speaks.

ACTOR 3: The year is 1992.

New York City.

East Coast Ode to Howard Jarvis. A teleplay. Based on actual events.

ACTOR 1: Interior shot, Rikers Island Jail.

In his thirties, African-American, jail guard uniform:

A Corrections Officer.

I guess I have always felt I pay too much taxes. Right? And I'm like, *for what*? Two days ago I'm like waiting *twenty-seven minutes* for a subway train, middle of the day, and I'm like, I'm *late*, I'm like "Come *on* man I pay all these fucking taxes like, for *this*?" For this *shit*? *Right*? Death, taxes and the fucking Mass Transit Authority. That *sucks*. That ain't right, right? I mean there must be more to life, you know what I mean?

So one day a couple of years ago at Rikers, I work here at Rikers, we got this weird skinhead white kid grand larceny assault or something, serious mental event, serious attitude problem, *nasty*, first day there he shoves some other prisoner on line at the cafeteria or he changed the channels on the T V without asking permission or I forget what but like so I have to take him to see the psychiatrist, get him some of them anti-aggression pills. I wait with him while he waits to see the doctor, and he's a talker.

(Beat)

Interior shot, Rikers Island.

In his twenties, generic white guy, shaved head with
stubble, tattoos, prisoner coveralls:

The Skinhead Inmate.

…this secret group which I can't tell you the name
of but to which I belong the initials of which are
N-A-W…uh… Wait, N-A-W. *(He mouths the words*
North American White Mens Freedom and Liberty
Council silently, gleaning the capitals as he goes, then:)
The N- A-W-M-F and L-C… And we have grokked
this shit but *profoundly,* like you probably *think* I
am in jail here but I am not in jail in my own mind,
like… That's *Thoreau!* Leonard, he reads *Thoreau!* And
he gots us some Uzis, we got Khlashnishnikov…
Klashkhalnikov…Kaklishni…whatever, those Russian
Uzis, and AK-47s, zebra bullets, dum-dums, Semtex…
Man. The free mind, the superior mind overturns the
system. Leonard, Leonard is like the mastermind, he is
so smart *(Confidingly, sotto voce:)* he doesn't pay taxes.
No shit, he hasn't paid taxes in twenty years and it's
legal because Leonard has proved through Thoreau
and shit like that that the I R S is unconstitutional. I
mean it man, clean and sober. No taxes. I have seen his
paycheck.

(Beat)

Exterior shot, on the street, Bensonhurst.

In his late thirties, Italian-American, tanned, pomaded
hair, gold chain, amulets, a police I D badge; he is
wearing a fancy Nike sweatsuit:

A Detective, the Housing Police.

So the skinhead fruitcake tells the corrections officer
this guy Leonard has found a legal way out of paying
taxes.

(Beat)

But apparently he won't give the officer this Leonard
guy's number or nothing because the officer's black
and Leonard lives out in Indiana where I guess there
are only white people, anyway, I mean who the fuck's
ever even *heard* of Indiana, I mean name-me-one-city-
in-Indiana-you-got-two-seconds-bleep-time's-up, five
to one this skinhead kid's never even made it out to
Coney Island, *Indiana*, Jesus *wept*. He hooked up with
(Making "quotation marks" gestures with his fingers:)
"Leonard" on the Internet. ...Now tell me please who
is it teaching disturbed individuals like this bonebrain
how to get on the fucking *Internet*, like when I first
heard the story I didn't even know what the Internet
was let alone how to *(Gestures again)* "get on it" but
here's this little cheap-ass racist loon got himself on
the Internet and he's cooked up this whole fantasy
about Indiana where allegedly they got something he
called The North American White Mens Freedom and
Liberty Council. I heard all this from a friend of mine
over at Rikers knows a guy who knows this guy who
got it from this kid: some bunch of armed whackos in
Indiana who had figured out how legally to get out of
paying taxes.

(Beat. He taps his noggin with his forefinger: "Bright idea!"
Big smile, shaking his head:)

MotheraGod. Gonna get me some of *that*.

(Beat)

Interior shot, a teenage girl's bedroom, Bensonhurst:

Seriously disaffected youth, hair in cornrows, dreads,
beaded, braided, dyed, mohawked, scalped; ear and
nose-piercings, tattoos:

The Housing Detective's Daughter.

My dad is always trying to win the lottery and shit, get
rich quick ideas, it's pathetic, like, you can just look

at him and see, "This guy is gonna get rich? Ever? No
way". I mean he does O K and all he just looks like
a buttwipe. He all the time implies that I am stupid
like he asks me what the Internet is. And he says can
I find some stupid group on the Web for him, like,
Dad, I am the first of my friends who found totally
naked pictures of Antonio Banderas, (like you can see
everything it is so *gross*) so of course yes I know how to
get on the Internet, buttwipe. Not to his face of course
but I know how to call him buttwipe with just my
facial expression so he can get mad all he likes but he
cannot hit me. Which if I *literally* called him buttwipe,
he could. So he gives me this piece of paper with
North American White Men's Freedom and Liberty
Council, so I'm like, "*whatever*". Buttmunch. So I did
some superlative prize-winning grass with my best
friend Karen and we got on the Web crawler in the
school library and fed it the name of this stupid group,
and *nada*, so we tried unlinking the words, like give us
anything with North plus American plus White plus
Men plus Freedom and of course there were a zillion
entries for that so like no way forget that so dad said
try "Leonard" which was so gigantically lame, what a
Cro-Magnon Pleistocene Pathetic Troglodyte Fossilized
Freeze-dried Buttmunch, but I told him if he gave me
ten bucks I would try "Leonard" so he did so I bought
some more grass for Karen and me and some brewskis
and some Camel Lights and she had some Ecstasy and
some crystal meth already and we typed in "Leonard"
and the Web Crawler was like, "Duh?" So we were
like, (*Throat-slitting gesture*) "DOOMSDAY!" but then
we asked this *supremely* scary girl at school who knows
practically *everything*.

(*Beat*)

Exterior, the front steps of a public high school in
Bensonhurst.

An African-American teenager, very cool, supremely self-possessed, dressed in perfect B-Girl style:

The Supremely Scary Girl Who Knows Practically Everything.

What the fuck is The North American White Mens'... Man, how the fuck should *I* know? Sounds to me like one of those militia groups they got out there, them Ruby Ridge head-jobs who got themselves all killed and everything last year, in like Utah or wherever.

(Beat)

Interior, teenage girl's bedroom, Bensonhurst:

The Housing Detective's Daughter.

So I told my dad who after all is a cop what this girl said, that these guys might be like terrorists or something, so he goes "So give me back my ten bucks." Pathetic, no? We tried Militias but there was a zillion entries, and Utah but again a zillion entries, it would have taken us hours and *then* because I am a genius and because I did not want to give him his ten bucks back I thought "Bombs, *guns*...light bulb!" So Karen and me tried Guns and got a zillion entries and then tried Semi-automatic Weapons and got a thousand entries and then "Semis plus Liberty" and got maybe forty entries and so that's how we went shopping for "Leonard" in cyberspace.

(Beat)

Interior, a high school library.

A teenage Latina, dressed similarly to the detective's daughter:

Karen, her best friend.

We found the web address for this North American White Zombie Psycho Brigade or whatever they call it, I forget, it was listed in this online 'zine called, um,

"Hyper-Vigilance!" or something. H-T-T-P-colon-slash-slash-W-W-W-dot-TEAPARTY-dot-com. So she tells her pappi she found it, and he gives her another ten bucks and tells her, E-mail them asking them do they know how he can get out of paying his taxes. And this dude is a *cop*. So she's goin', let's send this guy, Leonard "Hap" Dutchman, let's send him the e-mail, but I'm goin' wait, Sondra, you better come up with a better screen name 'cause you been using your real last name and these guys is loco crazy and you could get your pappi in trouble and anyway your last name is Procaccino and to these guys that ain't gonna sound white enough. So we tried to think up the whitest name we could think of and I remembered the name from off this book from school last year which no one in the whole class even bothered to read:

(Beat)

Exterior shot, an Indiana cornfield.

Generic white guy, fifties, fat, combat fatigues, militia cap, vaguely sinister toothbrush moustache, big smile:

Leonard "Hap" Dutchman.

Dear Ethan Frome:

Thank you for writing to the North American White Men's Freedom and Liberty Council. I applaud your interest in waging a counter-strike against the tyranny of taxation, imposed upon free individuals such as yourself and myself by the Zionist Occupation Government H Q'd in D C, its agents the Revenue Service and its armed forces of occupation otherwise known as the Bureau of Tobacco Drugs and Firearms and their elite corps the so-called United States so-called Marshalls. To *paraphrastically* quote our ancestral predecessor freeman John Paul Jones, "Won't fire till you see the eyes of our whites!" *(He laughs.)*

Having never before tested the tax-rebellion waters
as far east as Tel Aviv, pardon me I mean New York
City, I counsel initially a low-key tactical maneuver,
to wit: Request from your payroll office a W-4 form.
When you receive it, in the blank space provided
for "exemptions" write the number "98," hurling
all the while appropriate imprecations and oaths
against the high-handed shekel-mongering armed
moneygrubbering rug-merchants who force you
survilely to beg for "exemptions" from *their* usurious
theft of *your* hard-earned dollars. There's *no* I repeat *no*
legal limit to the number of "exemptions" a citizen can
claim, so claim "98," which if granted will effectively
and *legally* lift from your stooped but proud shoulders
the oppressors' contumely, also known as your entire
tax bill; and if your claim is initially rejected, repeat the
process several times, and if that don't work, Ethan,
E-mail me for further instructions. In the meantime
I will cyber-send you various useful items including
literature and a membership application for the
National Rifle Association. Good luck, fellow patriot,
oh, and Happy Hermann Goerring's Birthday, Mister
Frome! *(He gives a little Hitler salute.)*

(Beat)

Interior, a cluttered accountant's office, Bensonhurst.

A harried little Italian-American guy in his sixties, shirt
and tie, glasses, long nose hairs.

The Housing Detective's uncle, an accountant.

My nephew-in-law asks me is it O K he files 98
exemptions on his W-4, *what* 98 exemptions of course
not you idiot I tell him 98 exemptions you wouldn't
be paying any taxes, right he tells me that's the point,
I tell him listen Charlie remember Ernest Hemingway
you do not want to worry the I R S is after you, not
unless you like the idea of going down on a double-

barrel shotgun *(He mimes with mid- and forefinger the aforementioned act, cocks his thumb as if pulling a trigger:)* BOOM! Pay your taxes you're a goddam cop already what is this supposed to be a free lunch a, a, a free ride, *98 tax exemptions* what is you a friggin' communist gimme a friggin' break. Moron!

(Beat)

Interior, the payroll office at One Police Plaza.

A pleasant looking African-American woman in her late forties, early fifties, office dress:

The woman in the payroll department.

The first time I saw it I thought it was a mistake, or a joke so I sent it back. He sends it in again, 98 exemptions. I circled 98 in a red pen and a question mark and I sent it back. He sends it in again. 98 exemptions. I show it to my supervisor who between us is usually 98 proof before lunchtime, bottle's in his desk, lower left hand drawer. He can't even *focus* so he stamps it *ITEMIZE* so I send it back to the detective stamped *ITEMIZE*. I figure at least this'll be good for a laugh.

(Beat)

Interior, headquarters of the North American White Mens' Freedom and Liberty Council.

Leonard "Hap Dutchman.

Dear Ethan,

As per itemization, try our secret weapon: download and append the attached letter to your W-4 form. This document has proven highly effective by your fellow resistance fighters out here in the ZOG-free Liberation Zone formerly known as Crawfordsville. Please do not share this letter with anyone you do not love as a brother, nor with any women be they wives or mothers, nor I hardly need mention with members of other races. Happy hunting, Ethan, oh, and for twenty-five dollars you can obtain an autographed copy *(He holds up a book)* of my annotated edition of Mister Henry David Thoreau's survivalist manifesto *On Walden Pond.* God bless you and your progeny!

(He starts to sing:)

"BORN FREE,
As free as the wind blows,
As free as the grass grows…"

Cut To:

The Detective, Housing Police.

(Reading from a letter:)

To The Treasury Department:

Regarding Internal Revenue Service Publication 519 and 515. I submit the following statement in duplicate stating all my natural rights without prejudice in order to obtain work and not to be subject to withholding. I declare that I am an American man now in an area known geographically as New York. I was not born in the District of Columbia nor any possession or territory thereof. I do not inhabit the forum of your jurisdiction known as the United States as defined within the Internal Revenue Code. I am not a citizen or resident of any state or federal conglomerate within your jurisdiction. All remunerations for labor are received from sources outside the United States and are not connected to trade or business within the United States. Since I am alien to the United States, and am not a resident there, I am therefore a non-immigrant non-resident alien to the United States. I have never filed Form 1078 as prescribed that would rebut my non-residence status. I never had any income attributable to 26 USC 872 Subsection (a) Subsection (1) or Subsection

(2). I am excluded from having to obtain and submit an identifying number to you. Should I have any income from within the United States…

Cut To:

The Woman in the Payroll Department.

(Reading from the letter:)

"… I am still not subject to withholding of any kind of said income as it is not deemed to be income. I am not within a state or the United States, nor am I a person, individual or taxpayer."

Signed, Charles Procaccino, Detective, Housing Police, City of New York.

(She puts the letter down.)

The United States of America. Lemme tellya.

I read the letter a few times. Alien to the United States. Baby, I hear what you're saying. I am fifty-one years old. My apartment is a box. I got no money, I hate my job, I hate this city, I hate my cat, my husband hates his job, this city, the cat, we hate the disappointments, the delays in construction, the bigots, the bozos, the Democrats *and* the Republicans, Newt Gingrich, Bill Clinton, *his* cat, Rudy Guiliani, my insurance company and my boss, the guy playing with himself on the subway at nine A M, the kid with the radio playing at six A M and I hate the piss smell in the hallway that I have to inhale. Every day. On my way. To my box. Where I *live*. AND the fluorescent light fixtures they put up ten years ago in this office where I work that for ten years have been going *Buuuuzzzzzzzzzzzzz* all the livelong day like to drive me *CRAZY*.

I xeroxed the letter and I sent it to my supervisor and on to the I R S folks in Huntington, sent it to Albany, uptown downtown all around the town, put it in the detective's files, totaled up ninety-eight *itemized*

exemptions and where it says "Federal Withholding" I
entered "zero" and State Withholding I entered "zero"
and cut him his big fat check with no taxes withheld
and sent in on, let *them* sort it out it is *not* my problem.
You and me pal, aliens to the United States. I'd try it
myself; if I was crazy and stupid and looking to get
pitched in jail. But God bless the Child. He got his own.

(Beat)

Exterior shot, the Staten Island Ferry Terminal.

An Italian-American man in his mid-thirties, suit and
tie:

The Second Detective, Housing Police.

I thought he was just, you know, crazy or stupid. Then
a few months later he shows me a bunch of his pay
stubs: No Taxes Withheld. He showed me the letter.
I read it sixty times. I am a smart guy and I cannot
understand a word, he explains it sixty times and I still
cannot understand a word, I can smell *bullshit* when it
is waved under my nose but I cannot understand the
letter. I never been to Indiana, I don't read the papers,
I've never read Thoreau, I know nobody ever needed
an Uzi to hunt deer or whatever kind of animal they
hunt in Indiana so I don't know what this Leonard
character is up to but those pay stubs, *that* I can
understand. That is my kind of reading material. Three
pay stubs that read like that and I'm gonna buy myself
a motherflippin' Home Entertainment Center!

(Beat)

Exterior, night, in front of the giant Coca-Cola sign,
Times Square.

A Latino man, mid-forties, police uniform:

The Third Detective, Housing Police.

I sort of feel taxes are… Well people have been paying
taxes since…civilization, really, I mean since it began,
because, well, it costs money to, to *have* a civilization
and we don't want to be…um, barbarians or…I
remember back in the Sixties we… People talked then
about not paying their taxes but it was like… Well, the
war and all, different, different times. Plus which also
I am an officer. Of the *Law*. But. Well. By the time it got
around to me there were already six, seven, *ten* guys
all pulling in three times…well, *twice* as much as before
because… A *lot* gets deducted, so anyway. *(He shakes
his head, confused.)* I'm confused. Why did I? I dunno.
Seemed like a good idea at the time? Money pressure?
Peer pressure? Nostalgia? *(Leans forward, raises a little
power fist, speaks softly:)* Ho Chi Minh! Be Like Him!
Dare to struggle! Dare to win! Remember? *(Mimes
toking on a joint, makes a little peace sign, grins blissfully.)*
Remember that?

There is no force as great as an idea whose time has
come.

(Beat)

Exterior, underneath the El tracks, 125th Street and
Broadway.

An Asian-American man in his twenties, uniform:

A Transit Cop.

When Jesus says render unto Caesar that which is
Caesar's and unto God what belongs to God this is
it seems to me a very, very deliberately ambiguous
statement, Jesus is *carefully* avoiding specifying what
exactly it is which belongs to Caesar, or if, in point of
fact, *anything* really does.

(Shorter beat)

Exterior, the Brooklyn Naval Yard incinerator.

A Cuban-American man in his forties:

An Environmental Protection Officer:

(ACTOR 3 *enters.*)

ACTOR 3: *Me dice que hay cuarenta policias de housing que estan ya metidos, quisas veinte policias de transito, como veinte en Port Authority, E P O.*

ACTOR 1: *(Translating:)* He tells me forty housing cops are in on it already, maybe twenty transit cops, twenty or so over at Port Authority, E P O.

ACTOR 3: *Me ensena sus pay stubs. Era un detective en housing yo creo, es encreible, ningun impuesto—*

ACTOR 1: He shows me his pay stubs, he was, uh, a detective in housing I think, it's like incredible, no taxes.

ACTOR 3: No taxes! *Y me dice que me puede vender un packete que me explica todo, me costaria novecientos dolares.*

ACTOR 1: And he says he can sell me a packet, self-explanatory, it would cost me nine hundred bucks.

(ACTOR 3 *nods, then exits.*)

ACTOR 1: Interior, a locker room, Police Plaza gym.

A young fat guy in a sweatsuit:

A Patrolman.

I do not inhabit the forum of your jurisdiction known as the United States as defined within the Internal Revenue Code. I am not a citizen or resident of any state or federal conglomerate within your jurisdiction.

(*Even shorter beat*)

Exterior, night, Little Italy, the San Genarro Festival, colored lights, effigies, crowds, calzones.

A Precinct Captain.

I am still not subject to withholding of any kind of said income as it is not deemed to be income.

(Even shorter beat than the beat before.)

Interior, living room of an apartment in Washington Heights.

A middle-aged woman in brown traffic cop clothes:

A Meter Reader.

I am therefore a non-immigrant non-resident alien to the United States. I have never filed Form 1078. I never had any income attributable to 26 USC 872 Subsection (A) Subsection (1) or Subsection (2)....

(Almost no beat at all!)

Interior, Rikers Island.

The same corrections officer as at the beginning.

The Corrections Officer.

But what burns my ass is, like, I had to pay the mother two thousand dollars for his tax "packet" and I *know* it did not cost him no two tousand dollars to write "98" on a blank W-4 form and xerox this fucked-up letter that don't make no kind of sense. So why I got to pay two thousand dollars when half the force doing this and they didn't have to pay *nothing*?! That is not right. I was thinking of reporting his ass but then I decided against it, choosing instead to amortize the two grand as an unavoidable business expense spread over the course of two or three of these here Paychecks Blown Down From Paradise. Lookee this here! *(He shows the paycheck.)* Ain't that phat! I am taking my kids to Disneyworld!

(Beat)

Interior, headquarters of the North American White Mens' Freedom and Liberty Council:

Leonard "Hap" Dutchman.

Dear Ethan Frome.

We are pleased to hear that your East Coast rebellion is proceeding apace. I must warn you however against spreading the good news too liberally, if you catch my meaning.

Cut To:

The screen subdivides into many little boxes, each containing the smiling face of one of the officers we've met so far.

Cut Back To:

Mr Dutchman.

Because patriot Frome if there are too many non-immigrant non-residents residing in one location it could bring the wrath of ZOG down upon us all…

Cut To:

The screen further subdivides into many, many, many little boxes, multitudes of happy city employees who aren't paying taxes.

Cut Back To:

Leonard. Lines of static flash across the screen, the reception is faltering.

…and we do not I repeat do *not* want to face the wrath of ZOG before our tax rebellion has rendered it sufficiently cash-starved and weakened so the Council cautions you to….

Cut To:

The screen goes blank and is instantly filled with a notice:

THIS WEB SITE IS TEMPORARILY UNAVAILABLE.

(*Beat*)

Exterior shot, the Statue of Liberty.

An Sikh-American sanitation worker in a splendid turban:

I am a non-immigrant non-resident alien to the United States.

(Short Beat.)

Interior, Bellevue Psychiatric Hospital, a locked ward.

A middle-aged Asian-American woman, blouse and skirt:

A City Social Worker.

I was not born in the District of Columbia nor any possession or territory thereof, and my natural rights—

(Shorter beat.)

Exterior, outside a burning building, Upper West Side:

A Handsome Young Fireman.

I am not within a state or the United States, nor am I a person, individual or taxpayer. Thank you very, *very* much in advance for your prompt cooperation in ceasing to withhold my taxes! *(Smiles)*

(Beat)

Interior, a cubicle in the Office of the Comptroller, Lower Manhattan.

A young Latino man, glasses, suit and tie:

An Attorney for the City of New York.

Dear Sir or Madam: Please be advised that the status you are seeking as "non-resident, non-immigrant alien" does not exist nor is it recognized by any local, State or Federal Tax Code or Statute.

Cut To:

The Housing Police Detective, staring in open-mouthed incredulity.

Cut Back To:

The Attorney for the City of New York.

Dear Sir or Madam: Your request for "non-resident or non-immigrant alien" status has been denied inasmuch as no such status exists. Please be informed by this that you appear to be in arrears for Federal Income-, Social Security Withholding-, State Income-, State Unemployment Insurance-, and Local Withholding-*taxes*.

Cut To:

The Detective, Housing Police.

Dear City of New York: As a, uh, sovereign individual, who hereby formally declares himself to be a separate legal entity, one nation, as it were, indivisible, or rather, to quote from that classic of American tax resistance, On Walden Pond—

Cut To:

The Second Detective, Housing Police.

We declare that taxation without representation is unconstitutional and we do not feel represented by the governments in question and as it says in the Declaration of Independence which we spell I-N-D-E-P-E-N-D-E-N-T-S as in I am independent of your authority to request—

Cut Back To:

The Attorney for the City of New York.

Dear Mr Martinez Mr Austin Mr Yow Mr Shabaka Officer Vanuzzi Officer Vasquez Sergeant McGuire Miss Lefkowitz Detective Pentangelo Captain Russlowski Mrs Nguyen—

Cut To:

The Detective, Housing Police.

Uh, Dear Leonard—

Cut To:

THIS WEB SITE IS TEMPORARILY UNAVAILABLE.

Cut To:

The City Social Worker.

Dear City of New York dear State of New York dear
Treasury Department. I do not recognize your letter.
I do not recognize you. I am not a person nor an
individual nor a taxpayer. You have no jurisdiction
over me. Paying taxes is *voluntary*. Had I realized this
before I would never have paid any taxes, and I have
been paying taxes, before this year of my dawning
realization that I could not legally be compelled, I have
paid taxes for seventeen years: I am not in arrears:
YOU OWE *ME* MONEY!

(Beat)

Interior, teenage girl's bedroom, Bensonhurst.

The Housing Police Detective's Daughter.

So like H-T-T-P-slash-slash-W-W-W-dot-TEAPARTY-
dot-com was like permanently *fried*, so we went back
to Hyper-Vigilance, the online 'zine, and they had this
whole article about how Leonard had been busted in
Cincinnati for crossing state lines with a suitcase fulla
Uzis, and some bullets, and also he wrote some letter
to a U S Marshall saying he was gonna whack him or
something.

(Beat)

Interior shot, a maximum security prison cell, the
Federal Penitentiary, Toledo, Ohio.

Leonard "Hap" Dutchman.

(Singing:)

To dream the Impossible Dream

To love pure and chaste from afar

To strive when your arms are too weary...

Prison bars slam across the screen, Leonard behind them.

...To reach the Unreachable STAR!

THIS IS MY QUEST!

TO FOLLOW THAT STAR

NO MATTER HOW HOPELESS—

Dissolve under song to:

Interior, the Unites States Attorney's Office, the briefing room.

A press conference is in progress; behind multiple mics at a podium, a forty year-old woman in a power suit:

The United States Attorney.

Our preliminary computer check indicates that as few as five hundred and as many as a thousand city workers have been involved in this tax evasion scheme, some for nearly three years. Scores of law enforcement officers seem to be involved.

(Beat)

Interior, a Manhattan Court Room.

The Housing Police Detective in a suit and tie, looking haggard. A gavel is banging.

Detective, Housing Police.

I have no quarrel with his court, your honor. I am here against my wishes. I have no standing in this court. And the court has no jurisdiction over me.

(Beat)

Exterior, the steps of City Hall, Manhattan.

An out-of-doors press conference, facing mics and cameras, a shifty-looking snaggle-toothed guy with

furtive close-set eyes, a bellicose speaking style and a
bad comb-over:

The Mayor of the City of New York.

This isn't uh ideological. This is pure out-and-out
cheating. This is a way of cheating and not paying
your taxes by people who are sworn to uphold
the Constitution of the United States. If they were
ideologically concerned, uh, *political*, uh, that is to say,
making some sort of statement, they, uh, well they
could have quit their jobs, rather than try to cheat the
United States and the state out of taxes. They should
have just quit!

(Beat)

Interior shot, a classroom for gifted students,
Bensonhurst Public High School.

The Supremely Scary Girl Who Knows Practically
Everything is giving a report.

(Small beat)

The Social Contract. The Social Contract is a theory
propounded *(Big smile, she's proud of that word.)*
by Thomas Hobbes, John Locke and Jean-Jacques
Rousseau, who were French philosophers. Um, part
of the deal is, like, the people agree to surrender their
power to the state. Some of their power. But it's like,
how much? And it's like, say you the state and I'm the
people, did I "lend" you my power and can I fire you
if I don't like what you doing with my power, or am I
just born as a citizen alienated from my power, did I
somehow give up my power at birth and now I just got
to hope for the best from you, and um, oh yeah, like, is
this a contract between authority and each individual
or is it, like, a collective expression of a general will
towards civilization?

(Beat)

Interior, a plush law office conference room.

Set up to meet the press. A weary Irish-American man in his sixties. Rumpled expensive suit, glasses:

The Defense Attorney for the Housing Police Detectives.

But no, no, it's really not ideological, I wouldn't call what my clients did *ideological*, I— What's that? Uh, well. I would call it more like… Uh, well, idiocy. Or lunacy. Take your pick.

Interior, payroll office at One Police Plaza.

The Woman in the Payroll Department.

The day they announced they'd commenced to arrest those people was the day that T W A plane blew up and fell from the sky. I'm not a superstitious woman, but sometime there are signs, you know, warnings, you know what I mean, writing on the wall. Not that anybody knows how to read anymore, not that anyone's looking up at the wall to read the writing, but, you know… Signs. Trouble ahead. Oh, and Wall Street had a REAL bad day that day because the unemployment rate had gone *down*. That's what it said: the price of stocks fell cause there was too many people who had jobs. So I suppose that means stocks will go back up when enough people get fired?

My supervisor got fired, for gross incompetence, and I'm thinking of going for his job. Get my own cubicle, that way. Privacy. Maybe I'll start to drink.

Death and taxes. Baby…

I don't know what they're gonna do to those poor stupid people.

You could draw some bad inferences from all this. Things coming unglued. Can't blame the little criminals too much. Things coming unglued, that's how it seems to me. Don't it seem like that to you?

Everything's just coming apart at the seams.

And nobody understands.

Cut To:

Delivering the punchline to his 1996 State of the Union Speech before both houses of Congress:

President William Jefferson Clinton.

So I join with Congress and my fellow Americans in declaring:

The Era Of Big Government Is Over!

Cheering as the screen fades to black.

ACTOR 3: The end.

END OF PLAY

INTERMISSION

DR ARNOLD A HUTSCHNECKER IN PARADISE

CHARACTERS

ACTOR 3
METATRON
DR ARNOLD A HUTSCHNECKER

ACTOR 3: The setting is a beautiful room in a pre-war-Upper-West-Side-type apartment building in Paradise: rococo sculpted plaster ceiling, a small chandelier at its center, a handsome marble fireplace with Egyptian and Greek tchotchkes on the mantlepiece, books in oak bookcases and an old Turkish carpet covering a worn leather divan. This is the office for the psychoanalytic practice of Metatron, the Recording Angel, a vast fiery being with a million eyes.

Metatron is seated in an Eames chair at the head of the carpet-covered divan. Sitting, not lying on the couch—this is a supervisory session—is Dr Arnold Hutschnecker, best-known during his lifetime as the psychotherapist of Richard Milhous Nixon.

Dr Hutschnecker died in 2000. The play takes the year after that.

METATRON: And how are we feeling this morning, Arnold? In saying "morning" I am of course lapsing into poesy, since Time doesn't exist in Paradise.

DR HUTSCHNECKER: I feel lousy, frankly. I stayed up all night watching *The Sopranos* on D V D.

METATRON: Again?! Again with *The Sopranos*?

DR HUTSCHNECKER: I know, I know, I can't stop myself, I am obviously attempting some sort of negotiation: will the sexy lady analyst cure the gangster sociopath with narcissistic tendencies? It's that episode with the nympholeptic soccer coach, you know, Tony resists the impulse to whack the guy, her treatment is working! Oh, it's so tantalizing, so excruciating! She comes so close! He is borderline, not unreachable, I believe had Dr Melfi employed Pavlovian techniques, it reminds me of the early seventies, right around the Cambodia bombings, I, I.... *(Silence)* Oh forget it. It's not worth our time. My neck and my back are killing me.

METATRON: I would suggest that these pains are psychosomatic.

DR HUTSCHNECKER: You always say that, but…

METATRON: In this case my proposal gains strength from the fact that you are dead and hence you have no body.

DR HUTSCHNECKER: I'm not arguing, I spent my life contemplating the psychosomatic, especially as expressive of the narcissistic personality under duress. But my back hurts.

METATRON: Speaking of the narcissistic personality under duress, how is your patient doing?

DR HUTSCHNECKER: Who? Milhous?

METATRON: Who else?

DR HUTSCHNECKER: He told me in session yesterday that he doesn't believe he's dead.

METATRON: Interesting that you say discussing this television show—and I agree, it is superb, I watch it all the time, well I watch everything, I am the Recording Angel, it helps having a million eyes, I never have to channel surf—you say it isn't worth our "time", immediately after I have mentioned the fact that we are in Paradise and there is no Time here. Are you perhaps manifesting a denial of your own mortality, Arnold?

DR HUTSCHNECKER: Oh please, I lived to a hundred and two, in Connecticut, for pity's sake don't you think I was ready to go?

My leg hurts, and don't say I've got no leg. Look, it's
swollen. And I have hayfever, my face is throbbing,
oddly I never had it in Connecticut, with all those trees.

METATRON: The neck and back pains, these were his
presenting problems, were they not?

DR HUTSCHNECKER: Yes.

METATRON: Let's talk about counter-transference, then,
shall we?

DR HUTSCHNECKER: Dear Lord, that scarcely describes
it! When I was alive I saw him once, twice a year. Up
here, it's five days a week up here, five days a week of
Milhous, Milhous, Milhous!

METATRON: He still insists you call him—

DR HUTSCHNECKER: Milhous. MMmmilhous. Muh
Muh— It's so obvious I want to giggle, he wears his
psyche on his sleeve, it's always been endearing to me,
it saves me so much work, every day he comes in and
he says these remarkable things... Well, you know, his
mouth, oral sadistic, a few days ago he was thinking of
changing his name to M, just M, the initial he dropped
when he became President, and of course we know
what he's really dropping or rather who he's really
dropping or rather trying, still trying to drop after all
this...

METATRON: (Singing:) "M is for the many things she
gave me..."

DR HUTSCHNECKER: That mother. Her dying words
to him were "Richard don't give up. Don't let anyone
tell you you are through." I am afraid he has taken
this literally—he cannot die, mommy told him not
to. He has to obey, he must preserve The Idealized
Mother, the Saint, formed as he abreacts the depressed
controlling woman who couldn't stop him crying,
who breast-fed a cousin, a rival, when Dick—I mean

Milhous—was six months, who abandoned him for
mastoid surgery when he was nine months, who
gave birth to Donald right after that, more betrayal,
more abandonment, who left him in his remarkably
awkward adolescence for two years to go nurse the
dying brother Harold, more abandonment, more
guilt, well is it any wonder? What's amazing is he
did as well as he did, forget the Plumbers and the
tapes and the Checkers speech, what's amazing is he
didn't blow up the planet. *(Silence)* I think perhaps in
Hannah's obsessional, controlling personality may
lie the explanation of the fact that Nixon was the last
Republican President who believed in Regulation.
So she says "never die" and he can't afford to
disbelieve her, ambivalent mommy—combined of
course with his paranoia—and given her obsessive-
compulsive personality, paranoia's a…given. And
his religiously-inflected grandiosity, well he always
believed he was immortal—

METATRON: Masking of course a terrible fear of—

DR HUTSCHNECKER: Of course! *(He sneezes.)*
AAAAAAHHHHH-CHOOOOOOOO!

METATRON: Gesundheit.

ACTOR 3: Metatron hands Dr Hutschnecker a box of
Kleenex.

DR HUTSCHNECKER: Are you handing me this box of
tissues because you are suggesting that I am resisting?
That I should be needing them not to blow my nose
but to wipe tears away? That I am provoked by my
provocative patient rather than moved by him, I'm
maybe taking refuge in anger to staunch the inner pain
towards which this counter-transference is leading me:
my refugee roots, the rejection I felt by my motherland
in 1936 when I fled Berlin? An idealized mother, of

course, Berlin, Germany, my real motherland was—blech—Austria.

METATRON: Why are you sneezing? You can't really have hayfever, here where neither pollen nor sinuses nor—

DR HUTSCHNECKER: I know I know. He has a sinusitis flare-up every year, starting September 5 on the nose, as it were, and ending October 1. His father died September 4, his mother September 30. Ba da bing! Remarkable, as I said, I used to wonder if he'd read Freud.

METATRON: Have you ever asked him if he had?

DR HUTSCHNECKER: He'd say yes, but he would probably be lying, he lies easier than breathing—AAAAAAAAAHHHH-CHOOOOOO.
Well of what President could that not be said? They all lie, he's just so transparent, endearing, like I said, at least he wasn't overdosing on Halcyon, like Bush the First, at least he didn't upchuck on the Japanese Prime Minister, at least he speaks in complete sentences, he doesn't have a language disorder like the scary little stugatz they got in the White House now, and anyway I wouldn't mention Freud to Milhous because it could trigger an association that could lead him to one of his anti-Semitic tirades, I have a lot of trouble with that, it really interferes with my…
I tried to use Pavlov to get him to stop the war. Conditioning, behaviorism, that's what works with these guys, if Dr Melfi would… But that all went out in the sixties, touchy-feely and drugs were in and… The Manchurian Candidate. Have you ever seen it?

METATRON: Of course.

DR HUTSCHNECKER: Great film. I tried to get him to forge an association, "peace", "Quaker", "Mom." I

used to think Kissinger was thwarting me. Now I see it
was just the wrong series of associations. That mother.
Oh am I depressed. And I ache all over. Did I mention
my leg? Aaaah-Choo! Five days a week! Watergate,
Lincoln, that guy in the arena with the dust and the
sweat and the blood, undaunted etcetera and so forth,
you know, that Teddy Roosevelt quote? Jesus wept I
could sing you the—

ACTOR 3: Expletive deleted.

DR HUTSCHNECKER: —thing, he's been on my couch
reciting it for fifty years, and NOW! Milhous! Full-
blown stops-out week long psychoanalysis with Nixon!
Are you sure this is Paradise and not the Other Place?
AAAAAAAAHHHH-Choooo! *(He reaches for a Kleenex.
He begins to weep copious tears.)*

METATRON: His father was no picnic either.

DR HUTSCHNECKER: *(Through his tears:)* No, but that
mother.
He moves me, of course he moves me. Poor Milhous!
His mother couldn't stop him crying, when he was an
infant, she didn't comfort him, she'd stand over his crib
and say "He's not sad he's working on his lungpower,
listen to that strong voice, he's born to be a leader!"
Hence all the speechmaking, Madonn'!, the mortifying
rambling speeches, all the, the graphomania—he's
writing more books, did I mention that? —the sweaty
upper lip, I mean talk about psychosomatic! —and
what were all those words? Tears! Weeping! Milhous
crying, crying for the mother, crying out for hard-
hearted Hannah, crying out for mother love, for
America, the Idealized Mother, which heard but would
not love him and would only say "cry more, Milhous,
cry more, you are ...." *(He blows his nose and wipes his
eyes.)*

METATRON: Interesting, Arnold, what you said about Germany being your idealized mother, while your real mother, the bad mother—I believe you said "Blech"— is Austria, where you were born.

DR HUTSCHNECKER: Na, und? I mean, what's your point?

METATRON: Well, Arnold, I mean, talk about transparent. German ideal, Austrian roots, whom else might you be describing?

DR HUTSCHNECKER: I don't— Oh. Him.

METATRON: Ja! He always referred to Germany as Vaterland, nicht Mutterland. So perhaps here, the cause of your persistent refusal to consider the bad father introject inhabiting like a shadowy Cronus the cave of Milhous's unconscious.

DR HUTSCHNECKER: Huh. That's god, I mean good.

METATRON: So we may perhaps want to ask, in our next session, when you first elected to treat this man, this powerful leader, grandiose, paranoiac, anti-Semitic, often described as having a Napolean Complex... Who is it you have really been trying to treat, Arnold, whose anti-social impulses and abuses of power are you really trying to control? Who is your real patient, Milhous... or someone else? The one who drove you from your motherland in 1936? Are you perhaps attempting to rewrite history through your treatment of a less-malevolent surrogate who...

(DR HUTSCHNECKER *has fallen asleep, sitting up.*)

METATRON: Arnold?

(DR HUTSCHNECKER *snores.*)

METATRON: (*In a voice like seven thunders:*) ARNOLD!

(DR HUTSCHNECKER *jolts awake.*)

DR HUTSCHNECKER: Whoah! I must've...dozed off. I got to get more sleep, I think, it's the—

ACTOR 3: Expletive deleted.

DR HUTSCHNECKER: —*Sopranos*, I can't stop watching them.
That mother, it's just the best! Isn't Nancy Marchand here now? I'd love to meet her. What an actress! What a role! That mother! David Chase is a genius, I can't wait for the new season!

METATRON: I've seen it. It's marvelous.
And I think our time is up.

END OF PLAY

ONLY WE WHO GUARD THE MYSTERY
SHALL BE UNHAPPY

CHARACTERS

ACTOR 1
ANGEL
LAURA BUSH

ACTOR 1: The year is 2003. The month is February. The invasion of Iraq is one month away.

Three children in pajamas and bathrobes sit in small chairs in a neat row. Behind them, an angel is standing. Before them, facing them, a large comfortable armchair, unoccupied. Beautiful light.

The angel is, and remains throughout the play, unfailingly kind and polite.

ANGEL: Dear Children. Please rise and give a warm welcome to our distinguished visitor, the First Lady of the United States, Mrs Laura Welch Bush.

ACTOR 1: The children rise, wave their arms excitedly, open their mouths to cheer. The only sound they make is the bird music from Olivier Messiaen's opera, Saint Francois D'Assise.

Laura Bush enters, dressed in a purple plaid ensemble, carrying a book. She speaks with a gentle Texas drawl. She is a very nice lady. The children cheer and cheer. She stands in front of the armchair. She motions for the children to stop cheering and sit.

ANGEL: Sit, children.

ACTOR 1: They do.

LAURA BUSH: Why thank you children. I don't believe I've ever had a more beautiful welcome, really really lovely. But… May I ask?

ANGEL: Please.

LAURA BUSH: Most of the kids I meet when I visit for a reading program—and I do so many of these, I love reading to kids, I meet so many kids—but most of the kids are, are wearing—

ANGEL: They aren't usually wearing pajamas?

LAURA BUSH: No, they aren't! They… Oh well they wear uniforms! Or if they go to a school that doesn't require uniforms, they wear, well of course you like to see them dressed neat, I do, but you know they'll wear all sorts of things. Except P Js., I just never saw that before. It's sweet.

ANGEL: Perhaps this is the first time you have read to dead children, Mrs. Bush?

LAURA BUSH: Perhaps it is! And I have to admit, children, I'm nervous. I've never met actual dead children before. Nor actual children from Iraq. Before I met my husband I traveled all over, children, all over the world, and since we moved into the White House I have also traveled, but never to Iraq. So you are the first Iraqi children I've met and you look real sweet in your P Js. and I'm sorry you're dead, but all children love books. All children can learn to love books if you read to them. That's why I've come, to read to you, to share one of my favorite books with you, because when a parent reads to a child, or any adult reads to a child, even if that child is dead, the child will learn to love books, and that is so, so important. *(To one of the children:)* How did you die, darling?

ANGEL: In 1999, an American plane dropped a bomb filled with several tons of concrete on the power station near his village. He was already malnourished, he had been malnourished since birth, because of the sanctions. The power station that was crushed by the bomb was believed to be supplying power to a plant suspected of producing certain agents necessary for the development of biotoxins. We do not know if it did. We do know that it supplied power for the water purification system for his village. He already had gastroenteritis and nearly chronic diarrhea for which medicines were unavailable. Then the water purification system failed and he drank a glass of water his mother gave him infested by a large intestinal parasite. He died of dehydration, shitting water then blood then water again, so much! Then a trickle, everyone was sad, there was no food, he shook so hard the screws holding his bed together were loosened. It took three days to die.

LAURA BUSH: That's really awful.

ANGEL: Yes.

LAURA BUSH: Saddam Hussein is a terrible man.

ANGEL: Yes.

LAURA BUSH: *(To the child:)* Darling I'm sorry. I truly am. What a terrible world. May I sit?

ANGEL: Oh of course, please do!

ACTOR 1: She sits in the armchair.

LAURA BUSH: What can I say to you? Oh how can I say this? It isn't right that you should have had to die because your country is run by an evil man who is accumulating weapons of mass destruction. But he is, you see, he really is, everyone knows this and he will kill many many other children all over the world if he isn't stopped. So, so it was um necessary for you to die, sweetie, oh how awful to say that, but it was, precious. *(To the* ANGEL:*)* May I hug him? I just would like to—

ANGEL: I'm afraid not, Mrs Bush. The children aren't… ummm, they're incorporeal, they're like…shadows, or mirages, or dreams, it's hard to explain.

LAURA BUSH: And why are they in their pajamas?

ANGEL: Oh yes, I was about to explain. In Paradise, all dead children wear pajamas.

LAURA BUSH: Always?

ANGEL: Only pajamas, for all eternity. Bathrobes and slippers too of course.

LAURA BUSH: Well isn't that fascinating. Why is that?

ANGEL: Like all children in pajamas they are full of regret that their day has ended. But also secretly they are comforted, like all children in pajamas. Murdered children, the children who died especially terrible deaths—this child for example! *(She indicates a child:)* She was in a shelter in 1991. A smart bomb found its way down the ventilator shaft of the shelter. The smart bomb believed that it had found the ventilator shaft of a factory that manufactured parts for nuclear weapons, but the bomb was mistaken. Four hundred people were incinerated at a temperature of nine hundred degrees Fahrenheit. It was on C N N. Perhaps you watched?

LAURA BUSH: No, I... Oh my God! I did! I saw! It was green! Phosphorus! Night footage! I remember that.

ANGEL: Melting felt to her, paradoxically, like turning of an instant into solid ice, and then in the next instant like drowning in wild ocean surf, jumbled inside out, only fast, and then she was dead. Her family had been celebrating Eid! Children who die especially terrible deaths are given especially nice pajamas. Please continue your explanation. Mrs. Bush is explaining why you are dead, and in addition to being married to the President of the United States she is also a smart lady, she was a librarian! Please listen children.

LAURA BUSH: *(Softly, trying hard to explain:)* Because without sanctions there'd be no stopping him. And perhaps there'll be a war and many many more Iraqi children will die, and oh, honey, no one wants that, no one wanted you dead!

Oh God no, I mean God no what sort of animal would
want that? No, it's a terrible sin and I'm sure we'll
all have to pay for it, me and Bushie and—I call him
Bushie, my husband, I'm not supposed to do that in
public I promised I wouldn't but then he went and
made that joke the other day that I wasn't out on the
campaign trail for the midterm elections because I
had to stay in Crawford and sweep the porch after
it rained, and you know children I keep a very very
neat house and yes I do sweep the porch but he makes
me sound sometimes like a... A frump! And anyway
Bushie is a funny name, huh, a funny name for a
President, President Bushie? Without sanctions and
war Saddam will go on till he has the power to do
something unspeakable to another country, to the U S
or, or, well any other country, it could be anywhere, he
gassed the Kurds! So he must be stopped and you, you
were caught in crossfire and that is….
There's just no word for what it is.
And we'll pay for your deaths one way or another, he
just hates it when I say that, my husband, it's not in his
nature to think that way but I believe it, sweetie, I do. I
think there is guilt when a child dies even if the death
was in a just cause, and one person's guilt is guilt for
everyone—that's in this beautiful book— (She holds out
the book:) —and we suffer that guilt, me and Bushie and
Poppy and Bar and the U N Security Council; and you
suffered your death, all sorts of Iraqi people die for the
sins of your leader, for his evil, and you know some
people say serves 'em right but that's just vengeful
and, and indiscriminate and those people are wrong.
They're wrong is all, and (To the ANGEL:) how many
children have died in Iraq, you know, what with the
sanctions and the bombing and all?

ANGEL: The bombings of course have never stopped, they have been continuous since the Gulf War ended, it never ended.

LAURA BUSH: How many children, do you know?

ANGEL: Hundreds of children. Thousands of children. A hunded and fifty thousand children. Four hundred thousand children. Who's counting? No one is counting. A lot. From diseases related to the sanctions and the power outages and the depleted uranium dust shed from the casings of American missiles? Perhaps related? Probably related? Nearly six hundred thousand children have died. Many many children have died.

LAURA BUSH: Oh gosh. And on the bright side, all those dead children and yet look, you have maintained such a low student teacher ratio. Three-to-one!

ANGEL: We believe a low student to teacher ratio is necessary for learning.

LAURA BUSH: I agree!

ANGEL: And yet in the United States it's so high, on the average.

LAURA BUSH: On the average, thirty-to-one, forty-to-one! Way way too high! I was a teacher once. Before I married Bushie. Or, as I sometimes call him, The Chimp. You know, those ears. It would be nice if there was government money to make schools smaller. For living children. But you see, honey, sweetie, precious— do they have names?

ANGEL: They do but I'm not allowed to tell you.

LAURA BUSH: Why not?

ANGEL: I'm not allowed to tell you that, either. Sorry.

(Little pause)

LAURA BUSH: Oh. Alright. Well anyway, children, free educations with three-to-one teacher-student ratios or even twenty-to-one teacher-student ratios or even enough classrooms with enough desks to sit in would be swell, wouldn't it, but! One of the lessons from the wonderful book I'm going to read to you today is that if you accept free bread, or free whatever, education, daycare, whatnot, if you accept that free stuff you will have to give up freedom in exchange, and that isn't right. Freedom is what matters, not things of the earth. Like food. And I know you died starving, honey, but look at your nice pajamas! Do you see what I mean?

ANGEL: Children, do you see what Mrs Bush means?

ACTOR 1: They stand and answer, talking happily, but again the only sound is Messiaen's birds.

ANGEL: They really like you Mrs Bush.

LAURA BUSH: And I really like them.

ANGEL: What is the book you're going to read to them?

LAURA BUSH: It's my favorite passage from my favorite book, children, the book is a Russian novel of the 19th Century and it's called *The Brothers Karamazov* and the section I love most from this wonderful book is called "The Grand Inquisitor," well, it's a little strong for live children so I usually read them, oh, you know, The Very Hungry Caterpillar but I figured, being dead, you all command a broader view, and I hope you're going to like it. I think you will!

ANGEL: Who is the author?

LAURA BUSH: A reactionary Christian mystic epileptic compulsive gambler anti-Semitic Russian nationalist genius genius genius named Fyodor Michaelovitch Dostoevsky! Some people say he was the greatest novelist ever and I agree with those people, he was! I love him, I really sort of am in love with him, I think

he and I would have had a real understanding, he
wasn't so nice apparently but he would have gotten
me, I think, you know? What I go through, daily, in
my heart. Fyodor Michaelovitch Dostoevsky was
I think sometimes I think the only man who could
really understand me, and many many women feel
this way. At least in Texas we do. They broke a sword
over his head, Dostoevsky, then they tied him to a
post and over and over they were going to shoot him
for treason but they didn't, it was a sick joke, can you
imagine children, how ghastly, knowing, just knowing
you were going to die and then, and then…. You
open your eyes and you are still alive! Still alive! How
horrible! To be still alive! If my husband had been in
charge back then Dostoevsky would've been dead for
sure—my husband, he executed everyone they told
him to, everyone they let him I should say, my God,
a hundred-and-something people and he never even
missed his early, early bedtime nor for that matter
from what I could see as I sat up reading and rereading
Dostoevsky ever even stirred in his sleep! Notes From
The Underground, The Possessed, The Idiot and he'd
be all, like: *(She imitates a hideous bass snore:)* KKKKKKK
ZZZZZZNNNNXXXXXXXXXXXXXXXXxx-xxxxxxxxx.
Well he was tired.
He's tired a lot.
From the gym.
(Little pause. She is lost in thought.)

ANGEL: Mrs Bush?

LAURA BUSH: Well, anyway, in this section of *The
Brothers Karamazov*, an atheist intellectual, Ivan, is
telling his sweet handsome young brother, Alyosha,
about a poem he's made up, about Christ our Lord—
well not your Lord, you are probably Muslims?

ANGEL: They are.

LAURA BUSH: That's nice! There's nothing wrong with
that! But this is a Christian story is that O K?

ANGEL: Children?

ACTOR 1: They stand and respond. Bird music.

LAURA BUSH: I'll take that for a yes! It's a universal tale!
I bet it has been translated into Arabic, even into…
whatever it is you are speaking now, um, bird music!
Dostoevsky's Ivan, arrogant like all intellectuals, and
an atheist too, like most intellectuals he's an atheist,
they're mostly all godless, even the ones that think
they're religious, smarter they are the more godless
seems to me, but I don't really hold that against them
like some do, I mean this'll stay between us right but
don't get Lynne Cheney started, O K? Woo-OO! Ivan
tells his pretty young brother this story:
Jesus Christ has come back to earth, back to the streets
of Seville during the Spanish Inquisition, and the
first thing He does, well, this will interest all of you,
Christ immediately resurrects a dead little girl! Jesus
says "Sit up" and the dead little girl does, sits up in
her coffin, holding a white rose bouquet. But then the
Grand Inquisitor, this ninety year old Catholic bishop,
he's passing by and sees this miracle, and so he arrests
Jesus Christ and throws him in a dark filthy filthy
dungeon, with, you know, old rotten straw and mouse
pillies and, and the Grand Inquisitor says "I know just
who you are" —everyone recognizes Christ, somehow
they all just know him! "I know just who you are and
I am going to burn you at the stake in the morning as
I have burned one hundred-and-something people
already and I didn't lose a nickel's worth of sleep
over any of 'em." Some Christian huh? And what you
will hear if you listen carefully, children, is how the
Grand Inquisitor is really a godless old miscreant who
has abandoned God for the devil, who he calls "The
Dread Spirit" but it's the devil no matter what fancy

name you call him, and how he and his church, the
Catholics—and that's another reason I can't read this
to live American kids, is the Catholics are so friggin
touchy!—the Catholic Church wants to correct the
mistakes the Grand Inquisitor says Jesus made when
he was here the first time out. People want bread! They
don't want God or freedom they want bread! And they
want to be free of free will! And they want everything
to be uniform, universal everywhere, everyone just
alike! This is what the Grand Inquisitor says. Jesus
wanted people to be free, the Grand Inquisitor tells
Jesus, but people can't manage freedom so the Church,
and not just the Church but totalitarians of all sorts
throughout history are here to enslave them, feed
them, dictate to them, that's what the Grand Inquisitor
offers, freedom from freedom! And he tells Jesus
they will make a world, him and his fellow comrade
totalitarians, him and his big government buddies,
where hundreds of millions of people will be happy
fed slaves—they'll even be allowed to sin, a little,
just so they feel happier being slaves. Whereas Christ
would never manage more than a handful of followers,
only a very few would be strong enough to be actual
free people and follow Jesus whereas the Grand
Inquisitor would be leading hundreds of millions of
happy sinful slaves, every one of whom is proud to call
him or herself a Christian!

And because, because He was such a great writer and
this is such great great literature, when you read it
sometimes with all the "do-ests" and "thinkests" and
"wouldsts" and "thous" like in the Bible, and as you
listen to the immensely persuasive powerful tongue
Fyodor Michaelovitch Dostoevsky put in the mouth
of the Grand Inquisitor, sometimes—even though
I know the Inquisitor is the villain and Christ is the
hero—Christ says nothing. And my eyes start to blur
sometimes when I am reading this passage and I forget

who is the villain and who is the hero and I think
you know "Right ON Grand Inquisitor FOR GOD'S
SAKE WOULD IT BE SO GODDAM TERRIBLE to
FEED PEOPLE, AND AND IS IT REALLY WORTH
IT STARVING KIDS SO THEY CAN WEAR PJs IN
HEAVEN?"
And because it's genius literature of the first rank,
and not some magazine article, your eyes sometimes
reblur all over again as you're reading the twisty
words, and all of a sudden you don't agree with the
Inquisitor, he's the devil again, talking talking, but
suddenly something has happened and it's not the
people you are used to thinking of as evil totalitarian
people who are the evil totalitarian people who are the
pals of the Inquisitor and, well, the devil! You think
wait a minute, isn't this Grand Inquisitor starting to
sound like *(Whispers)* Dick Cheney, who just between
us—*(She shudders violently.)* Cuh-REEPy. You lose track
of who is who, your compass is gone all screwy, you
started out knowing for sure, and you end up adrift,
and the more you think on it the more the clarity of
the argument sort of melts like people in 900 degree
fahrenheit heat and all you can see anymore is pain
pain and more pain, like it's not about ideas anymore
it's just about raw naked SUFFERING, and...
And I know because, because I have suffered. I mean
he was right, the Grand Inquisitor was right, let's be
honest. It's too hard, the choice between good and evil,
it's too hard. Knowing it's yours. Yours to make. You
know all those times you betrayed God, you drank
and smoked and hated your folks or your kids and
you make a stupid little nothing mistake like everyone
else makes and gets away with but you don't, blammo!
All the perfumes of Araby can't wash the blood from
your poor little hand, who cares if everyone else makes
this mistake, GOD DOESN'T CARE, you are BUSTED
forever! Only, only a a a shitty person, pardon my

French, only a really shitty shitty person who isn't
a real person but only seems to be but is actually an
animal forgives themselves for…
The death of children.
But for those of us who aren't like that, we must be
punished.
Just between us.
And Fyodor Michaelovitch Dostoevsky understood
this, he wasn't snowy old hightoned Count Tolstoy,
no, he's down there in the shit with you, froth on his
lips and his thick tongue stiff, stiff and distended,
dear Fyodor Michaelovitch, the smell of cigar smoke
clinging to the coarse nubbly wool of his cheap black
suit and his foul epileptic's breath, and sometimes,
when, when I must suffer the touch of, of HIM. The
Dread Spirit in his newest disguise. Sometimes when
his hands are on me I say to my lonesome self Laura
Welch this is not The Dread Spirit who is touching you,
it's just dear dear Fyodor Michaelovitch Doestoevsky,
and he puts his whiskery mouth close to my ear and
he hisses Sinner! He knows, he's the only one who
knows what that word means! SINNER! I like children!
I really really do! Six hundred thousand? Jesus Christ.
A year from now, in what pit of hell will I awake!? I
was a Democrat when I was a girl! This is what great
literature can do! He weeps as he rattles me. I never
shall be chaste except he ravish me.
And I am rattled till my screws come loose, I am rattled
like, like… The way, when I am in a mood, I attack and
scour a sooty pot.

ACTOR 1: She demonstrates this: A wild, wild savage
assault with a steel wool pad on a large grimy greasy
skillet, one hand gripping the skillet like a vise, the
other arm working like a steam piston; growling, tears.
The children stare.
Laura Bush slumps.